ex libris

WINGATE-SAUL

....

TIBERIUS CLAUDIUS MAXIMUS
THE LEGIONARY

Peter Connolly

Contents

Oxford University Press

Tiberius Claudius Maximus
The Legionary

Lost in history

In the centre of Rome there is a huge column erected by the emperor Trajan. It is decorated with a great spiral sculpture telling the story of his victory over the Dacians who lived beyond the river Danube in Romania. The column has been standing there for nearly 1,900 years, a silent epitaph to one of the greatest armies in history.

Looking at Trajan's column is like watching television with the sound turned down. We can see things in great detail but we can hear very little, for the history of the Dacian wars has been lost. We can see soldiers camping, cavalry dashing through the trees, towns being burned but we don't know who or what. We know little more than that Trajan and his predecessor, Domitian, fought wars against the Dacians, and that in the end the Dacian leader, Decebalus, killed himself.

The Romans themselves would have known what these pictures represented. But 1,900 years later, little can be identified with certainty. We can recognise Trajan; his face is well known. He appears many times. We can see the bridge he built across the Danube and at the top of the column we can see Decebalus killing himself as a Roman horseman dashes forward trying to stop him. We can even see the emblem on the horseman's shield, but we could never guess his unit let alone his name – or could we? In 1965 a tombstone was discovered in northern Greece. Its inscription proudly shouts across the centuries. 'I am Tiberius Claudius Maximus of the Second Pannonian Cavalry. I captured Decebalus.' This is not all that the tombstone tells us, for it gives an account of Maximus' whole career. Using this and other evidence Maximus' life has been reconstructed into two books. This book tells the story of Tiberius Claudius Maximus the Legionary.

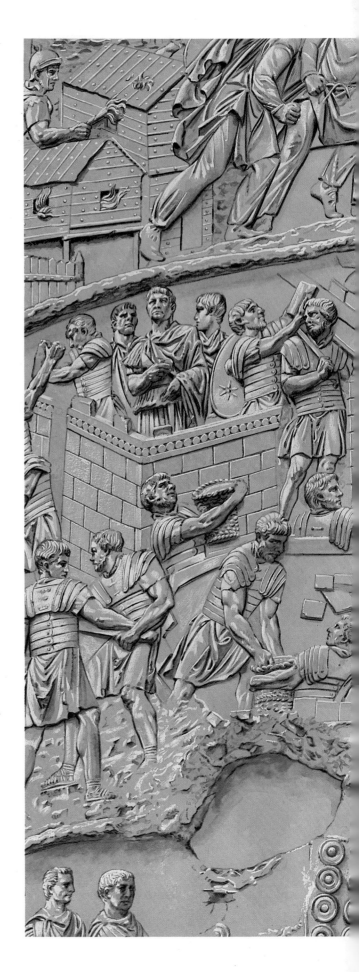

RIGHT: scene from Trajan's column showing legionaries making camp, as cavalry water their horses.

The volunteer

Tiberius Claudius Maximus probably grew up in northern Greece, near the Roman colony of Philippi. He joined the Roman army during the reign of the emperor Domitian (AD81–96), about twelve years before Trajan came to the throne. He enlisted in Legion VII Claudia Pia Fidelis, part of the garrison of Rome's long central European frontier.

This 2,500km frontier along the river Rhine and river Danube, had been established by the emperor Augustus (31BC–AD14), when he organised his own conquests along the south bank of the river Danube, and also those of his uncle Julius Caesar who had conquered Gaul (France and Belgium). Although Britain was added to the empire in the middle of the first century AD, the rest of this northern frontier remained unchanged for 75 years.

The emperor Domitian began Rome's last era of conquest when he invaded southern Germany in AD83, and established a new frontier joining the Rhine and Danube. His invasion started an upheaval along the Danube that was to last for 30 years. The Dacians living in the area that is now Romania, forced their way across the Danube and over-whelmed the Roman forces there. Domitian rushed in reinforcements and managed to repel the invaders. But he under-estimated the danger and returned to Rome leaving the commander of his bodyguard, the Praetorian prefect, Cornelius Fuscus, to launch the counter attack. Fuscus and most of his army never returned. Domitian hurried back to the Danube and launched a massive recruitment drive to replace the lost forces. Tiberius Claudius Maximus, now about twenty years old, may have been one of the many volunteers who answered the call.

RIGHT: map of the Roman empire in AD85, showing the Rhine–Danube frontier

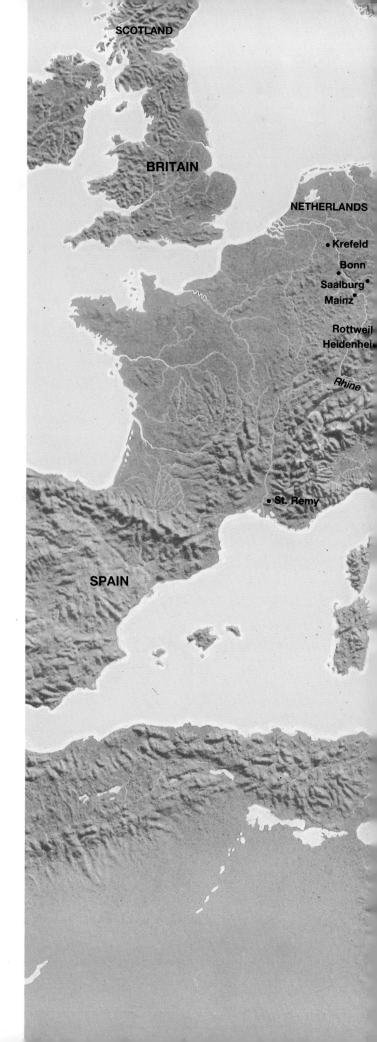

SCOTLAND

BRITAIN

NETHERLANDS

• Krefeld

Bonn
•
Saalburg•
Mainz•

Rottweil
Heidenhei•

Rhine

• St. Remy

SPAIN

RMANY

Vienna
Kastell
Künzing
Carnuntum

PANNONIA

HUNGARIAN PLAIN

Gherla

CARPATHIAN MTS

Sarmizegethusa

Tapae

DACIA

JUGOSLAVIA

Belgrade
Viminacium

UPPER
MOESIA

Danube

Adamkussi

LOWER
MOESIA

BLACK SEA

ITALY

Philippi

MACEDONIA

Hercuaneum
Pompeii

GREECE

TURKEY

Antioch

Dura
Europos

SYRIA

EGYPT

The new recruit

Maximus must have been at least 1.75m tall, slim but muscular, with good eyesight and hearing. These were the requirements for becoming a legionary. He also had to be able to read and write, but above all he had to be a Roman citizen. This does not mean he had to come from Rome. (He had probably been born in the province of Macedonia in northern Greece). It meant that his family had to have been granted citizenship, which gave them special rights and privileges.

Maximus' name suggests that his father or grandfather may have been an auxiliary, a non-Roman serving in the Roman army, who had received citizenship as a reward for 25 years' loyal service. In this case his family would have contacts in the army who could provide him with the necessary letters of introduction.

Those wishing to join the legions had to go to a recruitment office in the provincial capital for an interview and medical. Once accepted, they took the military oath, swearing to obey their officers and not to desert. Their documents, together with a covering note from the governor and travelling expenses of three gold pieces per head, were handed over to an officer who would accompany them on their long journey to the frontier. Maximus had applied to join the Seventh Legion at Viminacium on the Danube, some 60km east of Belgrade.

The emperor had ordered many fresh units into the war zone. The roads leading to Viminacium were crowded with troops and with refugees fleeing from the Dacians. Maximus and his friends were regularly stopped and had to produce the governor's letter before they were allowed to continue. Outside the base they were stopped again, this time by the duty cohort which was constantly on guard. They were escorted to headquarters where their papers were filed, and they were told the centuries to which they must report.

A hypothetical reconstruction of the Seventh Legion's base at Viminacium on the Danube.
The parade ground is behind the base flanked by the civil settlement.
A–A Via Principalis
B–B Via Praetoria

C Headquarters (principia)
D Commander's house (praetorium)
E Senior officers' (tribunes') houses.
F Barrack blocks (centuriae)
G Granaries (horrea)
H Hospital (valetudinarium)
J Workshop (fabrica)
K Amphitheatre
L Officer's platform (tribunal)

LEFT: scene from Trajan's column showing legionaries constructing a camp whilst auxiliaries stand guard. The main gateway is on the right.

RIGHT: a typical barrack block. It was divided into pairs of rooms. Each pair was shared by eight men who slept in the rear room and kept their equipment in the front room. The sleeping room was about five metres square, and the men may have slept in bunks. The much more luxurious centurion's quarters are at the far end.

The base of the Seventh Legion

We do not know when the Seventh Legion first occupied Viminacium on the Danube, but it seems probable that it was there by 85AD. The site has not been excavated. The reconstruction below shows a typical legionary base, with timber framed wattle and daub buildings erected within a grid formed by the two main streets, the Via Principalis (**AA**) and the Via Praetoria (**BB**). The headquarters (**C**) is in the centre with the commander's house (**D**) next door. The barrack blocks are built in pairs along the edge, just inside the ramparts.

Sore feet

For the next four long months the new recruits would be worked until they could hardly stand. They would learn to hate the very word 'centurion'. But at the end of this time the survivors would be entitled to call themselves soldiers (milites). Those who could not stand the pace would not be accepted into the legion.

First they were taught to march around the parade ground keeping in step. Then they were taken out on route marches and forced on relentlessly until they could cover 20 Roman miles (30km) in five hours. This was only the beginning: soon they would have to cover the same distance loaded down with their armour and packs. Those who fell behind felt the vicious sting of the centurion's cane. Each evening they crawled back to their billets, with blistered feet and raw shoulders, to get a few hours sleep before it all began again.

They were driven on day after day until they could cover 24 miles (36km) in five hours. But even this was not enough. They would not be accepted as legionaries until they could complete such a march in full equipment including armour, weapons, cooking utensils, palisade stakes, entrenching tools and several days rations, for at the end of the march they had to build an overnight camp with ramparts and ditches.

Originally the legionaries had used pack animals and carts to carry all their equipment. But 200 years before Maximus' time, the great general Marius had made them carry most of their equipment to reduce the size of the baggage train. The legionaries had been known as Marius' mules ever since. Full equipment must have weighed at least 30kg; their armour and weapons weighed over 20kg.

Legionaries went on route marches three times a month throughout their 25 years' service. Fully trained, they could outmarch any of their enemies; often a decisive factor in war.

LEFT: scene from Trajan's column showing legionaries carrying their food supply, cooking utensils and personal belongings (in a leather bag) on a pole over the left shoulder.

RIGHT: 1. Water flask from southern Germany.
2. A mess tin from Britain.
3. A cooking pot from Dacia. The last two are common finds and can be seen on Trajan's column.

BELOW: legionaries on a route march. Full equipment would have weighed more than 30kg. The Romans' ability to march long distances rapidly was often a decisive factor in a campaign.

What a legionary carried

Many details of military life can be found in the writings of ancient historians. The Jewish historian Josephus, writing c AD75 says that a legionary carried a saw, basket, pickaxe, sickle and a chain. This is a very simplified list; the basket and pickaxe were used for entrenching, but so were a turf cutter, mattock and shovel. No man needed all four tools. It is probable that a group of eight men (contubernium) carried the tools between them. Each man also carried his own food, cooking utensils and personal belongings.

LEFT: sculpture from Mainz in Germany, showing a legionary in the correct fighting position with his left shoulder into his shield, and his sword held horizontally ready to thrust into the stomach of the enemy. Behind him another legionary is raising his shield to receive a slashing blow from the enemy.

BELOW: recruits practising with wooden weapons against stakes set up on the parade ground.

Weapons training

Marching was only part of the recruits' training. They were put through a rigorous physical training programme which included running, jumping, and riding. They also swam in the nearby Danube. When they were considered fit enough, weapons training began.

Roman weapons training was based on the methods used by the gladiators. A hefty stake, the height of a man, was set up on the parade ground. This was the enemy. The recruits were trained to attack the stake with a heavy wooden sword, and a wicker shield which was twice the weight of a normal shield. Like boxers, they were constantly reminded to thrust directly at the enemy and not to swing because a slashing blow can be seen coming.

'Thrust, Maximus, thrust. No, don't attack the face. Go for the belly, always the belly. Go in under his guard'. The centurion's gnarled cane jabbed him in the stomach. 'Make sure you keep yourself co-vered with your shield when you withdraw. No, no, no. You leave yourself wide open if you rush for-ward swinging your sword. Keep behind your shield and thrust'.

Day after day, week after week they practised with their wooden swords, sweating and cursing in the dust. When they were not using their swords, they were learning to throw heavy wooden javelins at the stakes. Those who failed to reach the required standards were put on a diet of foul-tasting barley, and forced to do extra training, until they had proved they were good enough in front of the senior officers on the viewing platform, the tribunal.

At last they were ready to use real weapons. How light these must have felt after the heavy wooden ones they had grown used to. At first they practised against the stakes but finally they were paired off for mock battles, their weapons tipped with leather to avoid serious accidents.

Training recruits

Our knowledge of Roman training comes from a very late source, Flavius Vegetius, who lived about AD400. He wrote a detailed account of recruitment and training, in which he tried to show how efficient the old methods were.

Vegetius states that recruits were trained to assemble in the basic formations, single line, double line, square and wedge. They must also have been trained to form a tortoise (testudo), the most famous Roman formation (see *right*). It was claimed that the strength of this formation was tested by driving carts over it.

The testudo

BELOW a testudo formed by 24 men. The right side and the back were unprotected.

RIGHT: **1.** The positions of the four ranks.
2. The positions of the shields.
3. The second rank showing the positions of the soldiers.

ABOVE: scene from Trajan's column, showing legionaries advancing in testudo formation to protect themselves from missiles.

Doing the dirty jobs

The four months of basic training finally came to an end and Maximus became a regular soldier (miles). He, and the others who had survived, soon settled in to the routine of the camp. They still had regular route marches, drill and weapons training, but it was less often, and seemed a lot easier. They had some free time, but they were kept busy during working hours. Each dawn they reported to the centurion to get their jobs for the day, mainly guard duties, or fatigues like cleaning the bath-house or toilets. Sometimes they had more interesting tasks such as patrolling the roads, or doing police work. Their jobs were entered daily against their names on the duty roster.

Road building was one of the most hated jobs. It involved working in the quarries breaking up stones, as well as digging foundations and laying roads. Every new legionary dreamed of having a trade that would keep him so busy that he would not be available for the unpleasant jobs. There were many such trades including armourers, butchers, medics and horse-trainers. Such a tradesman was called an immunis. Several letters have been found from the legionary, Julius Apollinaris, to his parents complaining of fatigues. In one letter he is overjoyed because he has been made a book keeper:

> 'Now I can stand around doing nothing while other legionaries slave away all day cutting stones to build roads'.

A new offensive against the Dacians was being planned for the following spring (AD88). Viminacium was a hive of activity throughout the winter as troops and supplies arrived for the coming campaign. Most supplies were towed up the Danube in barges. But late in the winter, ice floating down the river crashed through the gorge to the east of Viminacium, ripping away sections of the tow path. It happened most years, as soon as the river subsided the soldiers were out in force repairing the path.

LEFT: the remains of the tow path along the Danube gorge.

RIGHT: the original tow path along the Danube gorge. It was supported on a narrow ledge about 60cm wide.
The cantilevered structure was regularly broken up by ice coming down the river.

FAR RIGHT: the new tow path constructed by Trajan. It was cut 2.5–3m into the cliff face to eliminate the cantilevered structure.

BELOW: legionaries repairing the original tow path.

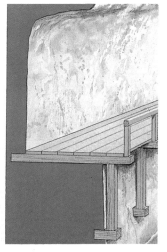

Fatigues

By an incredible chance, a duty roster has survived that may be from the very year and month (October AD87) that Maximus started doing fatigues. It lists 36 legionaries from Egypt, and gives their duties day by day. Among these are guard duties, patrols and fatigues, such as cleaning the toilets (ad stercus).

This is only one of many documents that have been recovered. There are also hundreds of inscriptions that tell us where a legion was, or what it was doing. Those in the Danube gorge commemorate the repairs to the tow path.

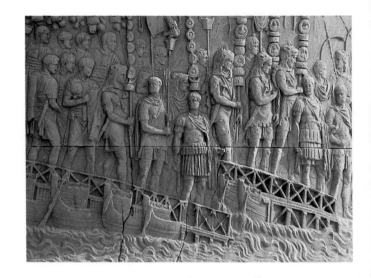

Bridging the Danube

As soon as the spring floods had subsided, the legionaries began building a pontoon bridge. This was the easiest and quickest method of crossing the Danube. It was also the safest as it could be constructed section by section working out across the river. The bridge was built on barges moored to crates of stones which were lowered into the river. A wooden roadway was then laid from boat to boat. The bridge was completed with a few days. Everything was now ready for the invasion.

The Dacians lived in the densely wooded Carpathian mountains, which have become famous as the home of Dracula. The Dacians were strongly influenced by the Greeks and reached a higher level of civilization than most of the other so-called barbarian peoples. Under the dynamic king Burebista, a century and a half earlier, the Dacians had become the most powerful nation in central Europe, but since his death the country had been split by civil war.

Dacian raids were a constant source of irritation to the Romans, but they had never been considered a serious threat. This changed about AD80 when the young and ambitious Decebalus came to the throne, intent on rebuilding the empire of Burebista. The attack across the Danube in AD85 was his first test of strength with Rome.

Being in the mountains, Dacia was difficult to invade. There was really only one easy route. This led north for 100km from Viminacium entering the mountains at Tapae. So Viminacium became the centre of operations against Dacia. As such it also became the seat of government of the province (Upper Moesia). Four legions appear to have been stationed in the area: Legion I Adiutrix, Legion II Adiutrix, Legion IIII Flavia, and Legion VII Claudia, Maximus' Legion. Legion II Adiutrix had recently been brought in from Britain; it had been stationed at Lincoln.

LEFT: a scene from Trajan's column showing Trajan's army crossing the Danube on two bridges of boats.

RIGHT: a scene from Trajan's column showing a barge being unloaded. This was the type of barge used for building a bridge of boats.

BELOW: fatigue parties from the Seventh Legion building a pontoon bridge over the Danube.

Bridges of boats

The Roman historian Arrian, writing about AD150, explains how the Romans built a bridge of boats. Barges were towed out into the river a short distance above the point were the bridge was to be built and allowed to drift down stream backwards. They were controlled by men in rowing boats who manoeuvred them into position. The barges were achored with pyramid shaped wicker crates full of stones. The spaces between the barges were bridged with timbers. A roadway of planks was laid on top of the timbers with railings on either side.

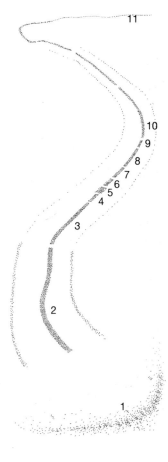

The Jewish historian, Josephus, gives the Roman order of march in his account of the Jewish revolt of AD66.
1. The auxiliary troops (light infantry, archers, slingers and cavalry) were sent out first to scout the area and search out any ambushes.
2. The vanguard: one legion supported by a body of cavalry.
3. Ten men from each century, carrying the tools needed for constructing the camp.
4. The pioneers who cleared the route for the marching column. They would remove any obstacles and repair the road if necessary.
5. The baggage of the general and his staff, with a strong mounted escort.
6. The general and his body-guard.
7. The combined legionary cavalry (120 per legion).
8. The dismantled siege weapons.

The army sets out

The auxiliary forces, those non-Roman troops who served as regular soldiers alongside the legions, began to move out of Viminacium at dawn. They would form a protective screen ahead of the legions, sending back constant reports on the terrain ahead, and uncovering any ambushes.

The legionaries rose and breakfasted at dawn. The new recruits, shivering in the chill morning air, awaited the trumpet call with a mixture of excitement and fear. When the warning trumpet sounded, they rushed to their barracks, put on their armour and strapped their helmets round their necks. When the trumpet sounded again they moved their equipment outside, loading their tents and all that they could not carry onto mules. They then fell in, century by century. The trumpet sounded a third time and the stragglers rushed to take up their positions in the ranks. The centurions now took over and marched them out onto the parade ground where the soldiers were drawn up, legion by legion, in front of the tribunal.

The army was commanded by Tettius Julianus, the governor of the province. He had risen before dawn to check that the omens were favourable and that the gods were not opposed to the campaign. He now climbed up onto the tribunal accompanied by a herald who spoke for him in a specially trained, loud voice. The governor congratulated the troops on their turn out and encouraged them, recalling Rome's many victories over the barbarians. He pointed out that previous defeats were due to lack of preparation and poor scouting. The herald then asked if they were ready for war. 'We are ready,' came the thunderous reply. Three times he asked the same question and each time the troops shouted back their answer, raising their right arms to stress the point. Then, legion by legion, they began to move towards the bridge, their pots and pans clanging behind them as they marched.

9. The senior officers: legates, tribunes and auxiliary prefects, with an escort of picked troops.

10. The other legions. Each legion was headed by its standard bearer (aquilifer) carrying the eagle. He was surrounded by the other standard bearers with the trumpeters behind them. The legionaries followed, marching six abreast. Each legion was followed by its baggage.

11. The rear-guard, composed of a mixed body of legionaries, light infantry and cavalry. The whole army (4 legions) would have stretched out for about 20km.

RIGHT: a scene from Trajan's column showing water wagons drawn by oxen and mules. One can also see horn blowers and a group of legionary standard bearers surrounding the aquilifer.

BELOW: the vanguard of the Roman army crosses the Danube. The vanguard consisted of one legion, selected daily by lot, and a regiment of cavalry. When the Seventh Legion was vanguard it was probably accompanied by the 500 strong Second Pannonian Cavalry, which was stationed near Viminacium. Maximus was later transferred to this unit.

In enemy territory

We know little about this war except that a battle was fought at Tapae which the Romans claim to have won. The Dacian king, Decebalus, must have known that he was no match for the Romans in a set battle, and probably tried to lure them into the hills. The Romans would have burned every farm and every village to try to force Decebalus to come to the rescue. This was normal practice. But they failed and the first year ended in stalemate.

The following summer the Romans tried again but this time they followed Decebalus into the hills, determined to invade the central highlands. The Dacians, now fighting on their own ground, would have continually attacked the marching legions, charging down on the Romans, swinging their huge two-handed curved swords, which were capable of severing an arm or cutting through an iron helmet. The army now had to march in battle order, constantly on the alert. Pitching camp was no longer easy. Every evening the leading two legions deployed into line of battle to cover the rest of the legionaries who built the camp behind them, with their weapons close at hand in case they were attacked. They cut down all the trees and cleared the undergrowth. Then they dug a huge ditch three and a half metres wide, two and half metres deep and nearly a kilometre long, piling up the earth behind it to form a rampart.

Each century dug its own section, which was inspected and measured by the centurions. Every soldier had his own job; there was no squabbling over who should do what. Some cut the turf to build the rampart; others dug the ditches, breaking up the ground with their pickaxes, shovelling the earth into wicker baskets and handing it up to those working on the rampart. The baggage train was moved up behind the fortifications where it would be protected if the enemy attacked.

LEFT: scene from Trajan's column showing legionaries building a camp.

BELOW: legionaries building a camp in the face of the enemy.

Entrenching equipment
1. Pickaxe (dolabra) and sheath.
2. Turf cutter. 3. Mattock.
4. Shovel.
5. Palisade stake. These are usually about 1.5m long. Number 3 is from Scotland. The rest are from Germany.

Digging in

The late Roman writer, Vegetius, harking back to the 'good old days' of the early empire, tells us how to pitch camp in the face of the enemy. Half the infantry and all the cavalry are drawn up in battle order in front of the enemy. The rest of the legionaries dig in behind this human screen. They dig a ditch 12 Roman feet (3.6m) wide, and 9 feet (2.7m) deep. The rampart, which is made with the soil from the ditch and faced with turf, is 4 feet high (1.2m). This would form the front of the camp.

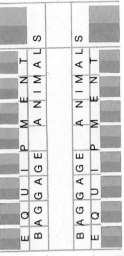

LEFT: the arrangement of tents for two centuries according to the Roman writer Hyginus. He allows eight tents per century with a larger one for the centurion. He explains that eight men shared a tent and that the rest of the century were on guard duties. Spaces were left in front of the tents for the mules and the legionaries' equipment. The centurion almost certainly kept his equipment in his tent. Each century probably had about twelve mules, ten for the legionaries and two to carry the centurion's baggage and equipment.

In camp

The ditch and rampart that the legionaries were building would form the front defences of the camp. Once it was completed, the rest of the army was withdrawn, unit by unit, and set to work building the other sides of the camp. Every legionary carried two pointed wooden stakes which were embedded in the top of the ramparts and tied together to form a palisade.

The fortifications were probably completed within two hours. Guards were posted along the ramparts and at key points within the camp. One cohort, about 500 men, from each legion was also left on duty outside the gates of the camp. The legionaries were now free to start setting up the tents. The surveyors had laid out the camp like a town, marking the main areas with flags. The site with the best all round view was selected for the general's tent (praetorium). All the other parts of the camp were keyed to this point. The camp had two main streets the via praetoria and via principalis. The via praetoria ran from the front to the back of the camp, passing through the praetorium, as its name suggests. The other street, the via principals, ran from one side of the camp to the other, crossing the via praetoria in front of the general's tent. These two main streets divided the camp in four.

Each legion had its own section of the camp which the surveyors divided up into a rectangular grid. Every century was given an area about 36m long and 10m wide. The positions of the centuries were always the same so that the soldiers knew exactly where to set up their tents. The general's tent was erected first followed by the other senior officers', and so on down to the centurions'. Finally, the legionaries pitched their own tents; at last they were able to relax and prepare their supper.

LEFT: **1.** piece of a leather tent.
2. wooden tent peg.
3. iron peg for tethering an animal.
4. wooden mallet.

RIGHT: scene from Trajan's column showing animals being led forward for sacrifice. Tents can be seen in the background with standards in front of them.

BELOW: inside the camp showing a large centurion's tent, and a smaller legionary tent with armour and equipment in front of it. Two soldiers are preparing to go on guard.

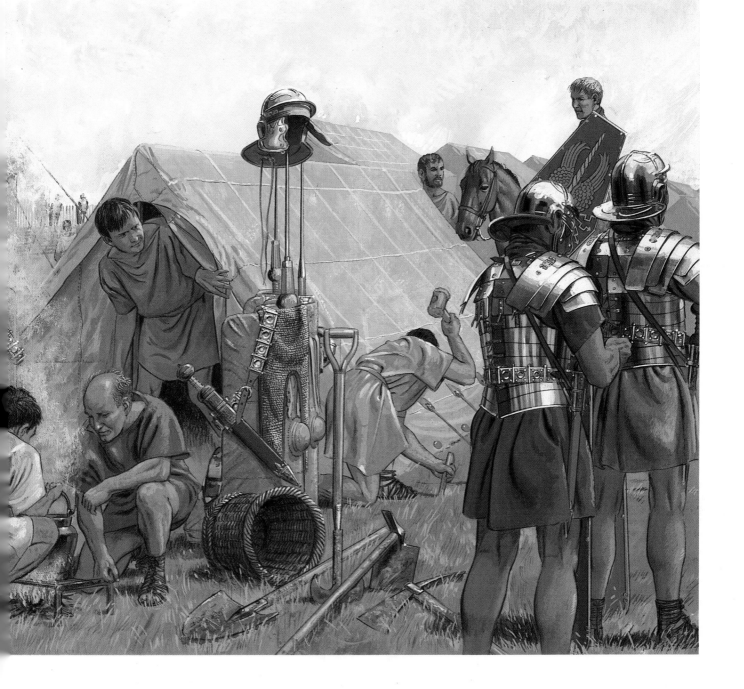

LEFT: legionary from Trajan's column wearing strip armour (lorica segmentata) and a cross-braced helmet.

BELOW: a legionary cleaning his armour on campaign. A fully armed Danubian legionary wore a cuirass of plate, mail, or scale armour, a helmet, right arm-guard and one or two greaves. If he had only one greave it would be worn on the left leg.

Decebalus decides to fight

A council of war was called regularly to discuss the problems of the campaign. These meetings were attended not only by the legion commanders, tribunes and prefects commanding the auxiliary units, but also by the senior centurions, the top professional officers of the legions. With their vast experience, they were able to advise the general on the practical aspects of the campaign. The dreadful injuries caused by the two handed Dacian sword must have been one of the items discussed.

The senior armourers from the four legions would have been called in. They must have suggested fitting the two iron braces, one stretching from side to side and the other from front to back, that appear on Roman helmets towards the end of the first century AD. It is not known exactly when this modification was made but it was certainly while the army was on campaign; the examples that have been found show how crudely it was done. It was a mammoth task. No doubt the blacksmiths gave it priority but it must have taken weeks to modify all the helmets.

Decebalus would have kept to the high ground, content with attacking Roman foraging parties and units bringing up supplies. Day by day the Romans penetrated farther into the hills, heading for the pass at Tapae which would lead them into the central highlands of Dacia. They burned or slaughtered everything they found, but Decebalus refused to come out into the open. The cavalry, far out in front of the main army, cut off any stragglers, sending back a constant flow of prisoners for interrogation. At Tapae, Decebalus halted and drew up his army along the hillsides, clearly determined to stop the Romans entering the heartland of Dacia. The Roman scouts raced back with the news. The legions reformed in battle order, placed all the baggage at the back of the column, guarded by a strong force of cavalry, and advanced rapidly on Tapae.

The tunic

The tunic was the basic garment of the legionary. Made of two rectangular pieces of woollen cloth, it was joined together at the shoulders leaving a hole for the neck. Sometimes it had sleeves and was stitched up at the sides. It fitted very loosely and hung down to the knees. The legionary wore a belt round the waist and hitched up the tunic so he could work easily. The neck was wide enough to slip out the right arm (see *left* number 1). When both shoulders were in the garment, the neck was knotted at the back to stop it slipping down over the arms (see number 2).

The cloak

The legionary wore a cloak made of a single piece of cloth, draped round the shoulders and buttoned down the front. It hung down on all sides covering the arms and thighs. The front was left open below the waist to allow the legs to move freely. The arm covering could be folded up on to the shoulder to free the arms (see number 4). The cloak was often fitted with a hood.

Foot wear

The sandal (caliga) was the standard footwear of the legionary. The upper was cut from a single piece of sturdy leather and sewn up at the back. It was stitched to a very thick leather sole studded with iron hob nails. Tests show that these studs wear down quickly and would need to be replaced regularly.

Armour

Trajan's column draws a clear picture of the Roman legionary equipped with strip armour, cross-braced helmet and rectangular shield. He wears nothing on his legs or arms. This has been accepted as a true picture of the legionary of this period. However, there is a monument at Adamklissi in Romania which tells a very different story. It shows legionaries with rectangular shields and cross-braced helmets, but they are wearing mail and scale shirts, arm guards and greaves. Clearly there was a greater variety of equipment.

ABOVE: **1.** legionary from Trajan's column working with his right arm bare.
2. legionary from Trajan's column working with his tunic knotted at the back of the neck.
3. statue of a legionary found in London, showing the military cloak folded up over the right shoulder.

BELOW: typical Roman military sandal (caliga) found in Britain.

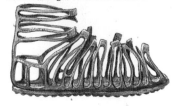

ABOVE: legionary shown on the Adamklissi monument.

Helmets

Three cross-braced helmets have been found in the Danube region. They are typical of the iron helmets made in the Rhineland in the second half of the first century AD, except that they have rough iron braces riveted on to them. The way the iron braces cross straight over the decoration shows that they were fitted as an after-thought.

These helmets were padded on the inside, and had straps attached by rings to the broad neck-guard. The straps were pulled forward and crossed at the throat. They were then threaded through rings inside the cheek-pieces and tied under the chin. This made it almost impossible for the helmet to come off.

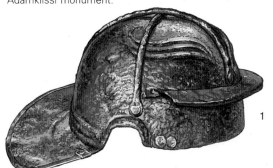

ABOVE: **1.** cross-braced helmet from Romania.
2. typical cheek-piece.
3. how the cross-braces were fitted to a typical Rhineland helmet.

Armour and Weapons

Pieces of lorica segmentata found at Corbridge, England.
1. left upper back unit.
2. left chest/shoulder unit.
3. left 3-part shoulder plate.

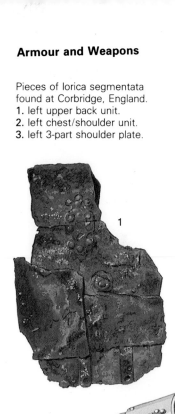

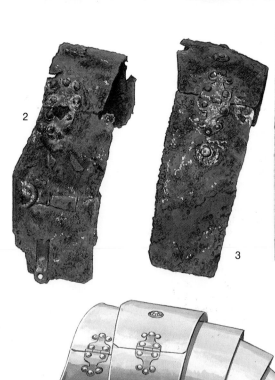

ABOVE: the Tyne shield boss. Scale 1:5. with three sections to show the curve of the shield.

BELOW: a reconstructed scutum based on the example from Dura Europos in Syria.

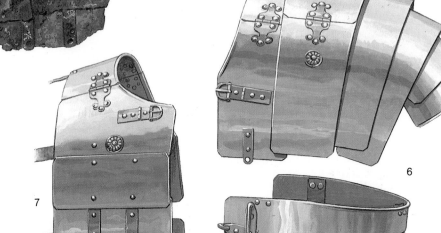

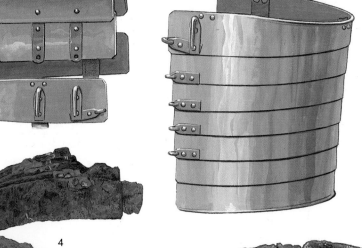

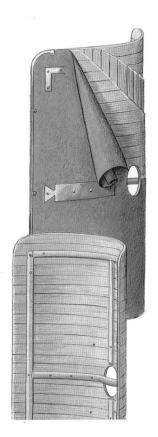

4. girdle plates from back.
5. girdle plates from front.
6. reconstruction of left side of the armour – front view.
7. reconstruction of left upper back unit

Body armour

There were three types of body armour, mail (linked rings), scale, and plate armour. Iron scales were found at the legionary base at Carnuntum on the Danube. Some were more than 4cm long and 1mm thick. They overlapped in such a way that the armour was always two scales thick.

Plate armour

A number of iron plates with bronze fittings were also found at Carnuntum, showing that plate armour was also in use along the Danube. The best examples of this type of armour (lorica segmentata) come from Corbridge in northern Britain, where three complete sets were found. These survived complete with the leather straps, on which the plates were suspended.

Shields

The shield (scutum) was made of strips of wood glued together like three-ply wood and covered with hide or felt. It was about 1m long, and curved. The curve is illustrated by the shield boss found in the Tyne (see page 25). The three sections vary a little. The centre one corresponds with a circle just under 1m in diameter. The shield weighed about 6kg.

Weapons

The legionary was armed with a javelin (pilum), dagger (pugio) and sword (gladius). Three almost complete pila were found at Oberraden in northern Germany; only the lower parts are missing. They have a thin iron shaft, about 60cm long, with a pyramid-shaped point and a flat tang (see number **4**). The tang is slotted into the wooden handle and held in place by three rivets. Two other types of pila are often found. They differ only in the way the head is fixed to the wooden shaft (number **2** and **3**). The Oberraden pila weigh only about 1kg. A heavier pilum, with a lead weight just above the handgrip, was introduced shortly before Maximus entered the army.

The dagger

The dagger was a short weapon with a long-pointed blade about 25cm in length. The scabbard was made of wood, faced with a decorated bronze plate.

The sword

The sword was a short straight-edged weapon with a blade 40–50cm long. One of these was recently found at Herculaneum, a town destroyed when Vesuvius erupted in AD79. Its scabbard, two belts and the apron straps, that hung down the front, were found with it. These were in use just six or seven years before Maximus entered the army. The examples below are from Jugoslavia, where the Seventh Legion was stationed. They are almost identical to those found at Herculaneum.

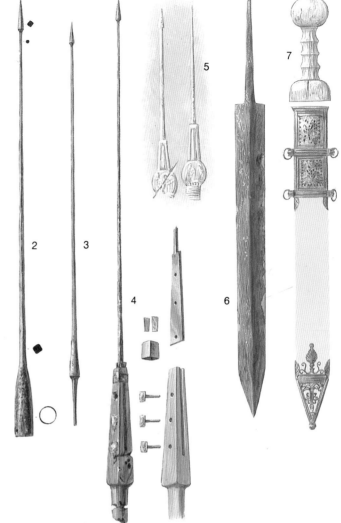

LEFT: **1.** dagger and scabbard plate from Mainz, Germany.

BELOW: belt and apron fittings from Jugoslavia.
8. belt plate with buckle.
9. belt plate with dagger clasp.
10 & 11. apron strap ends.
12. disc from an apron strap.

ABOVE: **2 & 3** socketed and tanged pilum heads from the Saalburg, Germany.
4. one of the pila from Oberraden, Germany
5. weighted pila shown on the Cancelleria relief at Rome.
6. sword blade from Newstead, Scotland.
7. sword fittings from various sites. All one sixth of actual size.

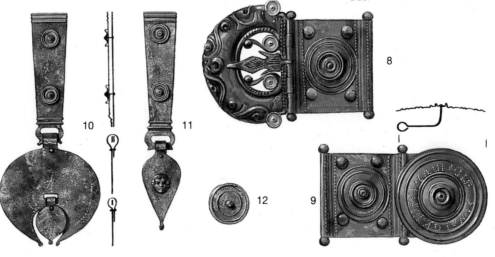

25

The battle begins

The Romans advanced to within 4km of the Dacian position, and deployed the first two legions into battle line with the auxiliary forces on either side. The rest of the legionaries put aside their shields, helmets and weapons, keeping them within easy reach, and began to dig in. All the camp servants, traders and others who were following the army, crowded in behind the ditch with the baggage and siege weapons. This was normal practice.

We have no idea what happened next. Maybe the Dacians attacked while the Romans were digging in. It seems likely, for the Romans were most vulnerable at this moment. The idea of a set battle with both armies drawn up opposite each other on open ground is attractive, but it seldom happened, especially when fighting barbarians. Julius Caesar's military career lasted 14 years, but he only fought one such battle in all that time; that was against another Roman, Pompey the Great.

One can imagine the situation; the Dacians are massed along the hillsides with their multi-coloured dragon standards fluttering overhead. They are screaming insults at the Romans amidst raucous blasts from their war trumpets. Suddenly they seem to realize that only part of the Roman army is actually facing them, and the whole mass surges down the hillside with a thunderous roar.

The trumpets sound the call to arms. Those working in the ditch grab their weapons and run to join their standards, fumbling as they try to remove the leather covers from their shields. The disciplined legionaries already in battle order stand motionless. Only their right hands move as they rattle their heavy javelins against their shields, the unearthly sound echoing along the hills like rumbling thunder. At last, when the enemy are almost upon them, the trumpets sound the charge and the legionaries dash forward with a mighty roar hurling their javelins into the screaming horde.

LEFT: scene from Trajan's column showing a prisoner being brought in for questioning.

RIGHT: scene from Trajan's column showing Dacians fighting Roman auxiliary troops.

BELOW: legionaries throwing their javelins to break up the Dacian charge.

The heavy javelin

The Roman use of the heavy javelin (pilum), and the short thrusting sword, was a unique combination. The pilum was probably introduced in the fourth century BC to break up the ferocious Celtic charge. It was a very effective weapon; no army could maintain both its momentum and its formation when faced with a hail of these weapons. Polybius, the Greek historian writing about 150BC, states that each legionary carried two javelins, one thick and the other slim. This description fits the flat-tanged and socketed types that are found (see p25).

BELOW: in the confusion caused by the hail of heavy javelins, the Romans draw their short swords and charge into the Dacians.

RIGHT: **1.** Dacian with a two-handed curved sword (falx) from the Adamlissi monument.
2. Dacian falx 90cm long.
FAR RIGHT: scene from Trajan's column showing a first aid station.

First blood

The murderous hail of javelins caused havoc, particularly amongst those with two-handed swords, for without shields or body armour, they were an open target. They tried desperately to avoid the javelins, but with so many coming at once, it was almost impossible. Some, unable to get out of the way, tried to catch them and throw them back. Those with shields fared a lot better, but when a javelin became stuck in a shield, its thin iron shaft buckled, making the shield too unwieldy to use.

The force of the Dacian charge was broken. The legionaries, drawing their swords in the confusion, dashed in to close quarters. They threw their whole weight against the Dacians, trying to knock them off balance. The battle now became a test of skill, stamina and discipline as the recruits put their training to the test.

It was now that the hated centurions showed their true character, for as the young and inexperienced recruits broke ranks before the dreaded Dacian swordsmen, the centurions stood their ground, ready to sacrifice their lives to save their men. Maximus suddenly heard the man he hated encouraging him and urging him on. For the first time he saw the real man behind the harsh facade.

'Come on Maximus. He's only a barbarian. Remember what I taught you. Go for his belly'.
Maximus saw a massive Dacian towering over him, curved sword high above his head. He raised his shield instinctively. The force of the blow almost dislocated his shoulder. A shower of splinters hit him in the face, momentarily blinding him. He could hear the centurion's voice:

'Go for the belly. Thrust, Maximus, thrust'.
He lunged forward as he had been trained and felt his sword cut into something soft. He heard a groan and felt warm blood on his hand ... This may be fiction, but we know that Maximus was decorated for his courage.

1

2

The centurions

The true character of the centurions is well illustrated by an episode from Caesar's Gallic War. In 52BC Caesar's troops tried to storm the hillfort of Gergovia. They failed and were driven back down the hill. Casualties might have been very high but the centurions stood their ground covering the retreat of their men. Nearly 700 men were killed of which 46 were centurions – one centurion for every 14 legionaries. The normal ratio is 1:80.

Legion Organisation and Promotion

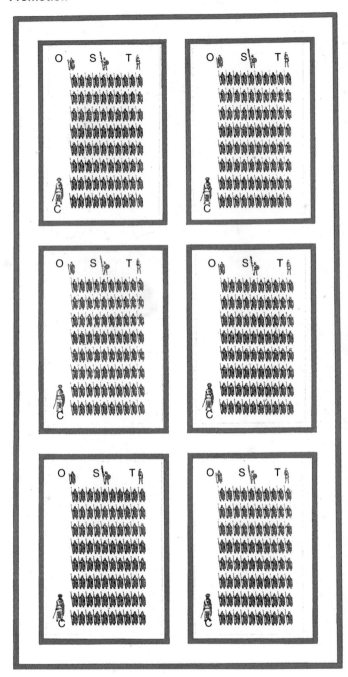

No more fatigues

Battered but unbeaten, the Dacians withdrew to the high ground. The Romans had no desire to continue the campaign. The enemy had been seen to be punished, and morale was restored. A few days later the Romans broke camp and returned to the Danube.

Maximus would have soon settled into the routine of camp life again. It was not all drill and fatigues. The legionaries had plenty of free time which they spent in the town or relaxing at the baths. We know nothing of Maximus' private life. Soldiers were forbidden to marry, but he must have met many of the local girls and may even have formed a permanent relationship with one of them. Their children would not have been legitimate but that could be put right when he retired. Such common law marriages are well known from soldiers' letters found in Egypt.

Maximus' tombstone tells us a great deal about his military career. Somehow he got himself transferred to the legion's 120 strong cavalry unit, which probably removed his name from the general fatigues roster. As a cavalryman, he would have spent much of his working life on patrol or dispatch riding along the Danube. In time he rose to be banker for his new unit, a testimony of his honesty, and was selected for the commander's mounted bodyguard. Finally he was promoted to standard bearer with double pay. His next promotion would have been to centurion but for some reason he never made it. An expeditionary force was sent across Dacia to southern Germany shortly after the war, but we have no way of knowing whether Maximus was involved. It may have been a dozen years later before he saw active service again. The next thing we know is that he was transferred to an independent cavalry unit by the emperor Trajan. But that is the subject of another book:
Tiberius Claudius Maximus the cavalryman

ABOVE: a standard cohort with six normal size centuries.
C centurion. O optio.
S standard bearer (signifer).
T tesserarius.

BELOW: a legion composed of nine standard cohorts of about 480 men each, one large cohort of about 800 men and 120 cavalry.

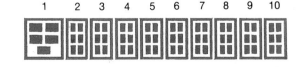

Composition of the legion

The legion was made up of ten cohorts. Nine of these, cohorts 2–10, were composed of six centuries, each containing about 80 men. Each century commanded by a centurion had its own standard. The centurion had a second in command (optio) and an orderly (tesserarius).

The first cohort

The first cohort was composed of five double centuries each commanded by a centurion. These were the top centurions of the legion (primi ordines), the most senior being the primus pilus, who was entitled to attend the council of war.

The legionary cavalry

The legion also had 120 cavalry (equites legionis), used as dispatch riders and cavalry escort for the commander.

Command

The legion was commanded by a legate, assisted by six tribunes. These were sent out by Rome and were not professional soldiers.

Promotion

Maximus probably started as a foot soldier (miles), although this is not mentioned on his tombstone. Normally a recruit spent several years as a foot soldier before promotion to the legionary cavalry.

First advancement for a miles would be to immunis with a trade such as clerk or blacksmith. This took him off the roster of soldiers available for general duties.

An immunis received no more pay than a miles, but a cavalryman got extra, probably for the upkeep of his horse.

Principales

First real promotion was to the principales who were split into two groups: those on pay and a half (sesquiplicarii), and those on double pay (duplicarii). Pay-and-a-half men included junior staff officers such as tesserarius, and quaestor equitum. Among the double-pay men were standard bearers (signiferi and vexillarii), optiones and other senior officers. The next promotion was to centurion.

Maximus' tombstone

The inset picture at the top shows Maximus on horseback with Decebalus underneath. Below are two torques and bracelets (armillae), probably the decorations he won at Tapae. The inscription is written in abbreviated Latin. The full text would read:
Tiberius Claudius Maximus, veteranus sibi vivo faciendum curavit. Militavit eques in legione VII Claudia pia fideli, factus quaestor equitum, singularis legati legionis eiusdem, vexillarius equitum, item bello Dacico ob virtutem donis donatus ab imperatore Domitiano.
In brief it says that he was a veteran (*veteranus*) of the Seventh Legion where he served as a cavalryman (*eques*). He became banker for his unit (*quaestor equitum*), bodyguard of the legion commander (*singularis legati legionis*), standard bearer of the legionary cavalry (*vexillarius equitum*), and in the Dacian war (*bello Dacico*) for his bravery (*virtutem*) was given 'medals' (*donis*) by the emperor Domitian. The tombstone goes on to record his career under the emperor Trajan.

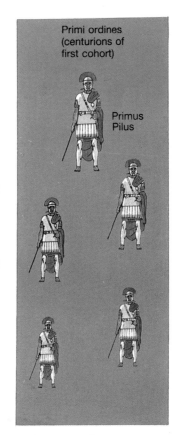

Primi ordines (centurions of first cohort)

Primus Pilus

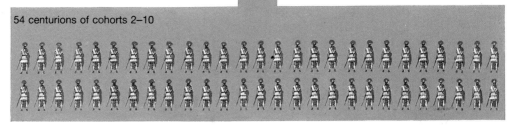

54 centurions of cohorts 2–10

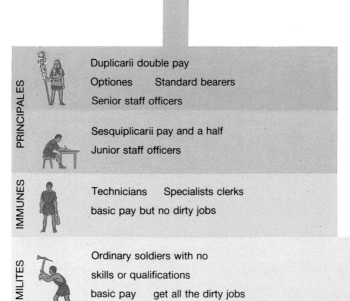

EQUITES

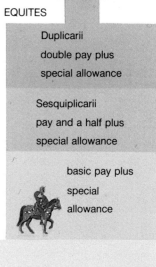

PRINCIPALES
Duplicarii double pay
Optiones   Standard bearers
Senior staff officers

Sesquiplicarii pay and a half
Junior staff officers

IMMUNES
Technicians   Specialists clerks
basic pay but no dirty jobs

MILITES
Ordinary soldiers with no skills or qualifications
basic pay   get all the dirty jobs

EQUITES
Duplicarii
double pay plus
special allowance

Sesquiplicarii
pay and a half plus
special allowance

basic pay plus
special
allowance

Index

Peter Connolly is an honorary research fellow of the Institute of Archaeology, University College, London, and a fellow of the Society of Antiquaries. He is the author and illustrator of *The Roman Army*, *The Greek Armies*, *Hannibal and the Enemies of Rome*, *Pompeii*, *Greece and Rome at War*, *Living in the time of Jesus of Nazareth*, and *The Legend of Odysseus* for which he won *The Times Educational Supplement* Information Book Award.

The author wishes to thank Dr Brian Dobson of Durham University, and Mr Mark Hassall of the Institute of Archaeology, University College, London for their advice and help in checking the manuscript and illustrations. He would also like to thank Dr Margaret Roxan, Dr David Breeze and Professor John Mann for their advice.

Oxford University Press, Walton Street, Oxford OX2 6DP

Oxford New York Toronto
Delhi Bombay Calcutta Madras Karachi
Petaling Jaya Singapore Hong Kong Tokyo
Nairobi Dar es Salaam Cape Town

and associated companies in
Berlin Ibadan

Oxford is a trade mark of Oxford University Press

First published in the United States in 1989
Reprinted 1991
Library of Congress catalog card number 88-043212.

ISBN 0 19 917105 X

Phototypeset by Tradespools Ltd, Frome, Somerset
Printed in Hong Kong